Animals of Africa
GAZELLES

by Tammy Gagne

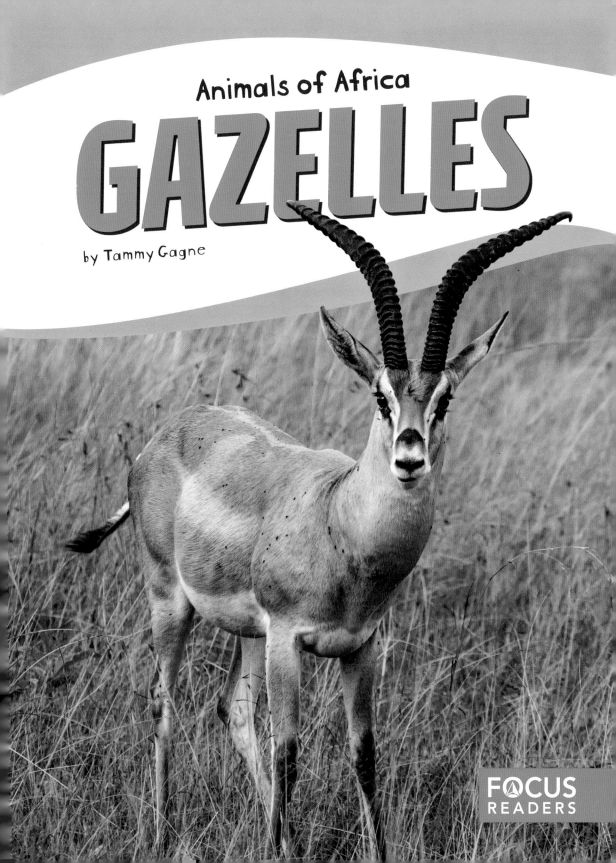

FOCUS READERS

www.focusreaders.com

Focus Readers is distributed by North Star Editions:
sales@northstareditions.com | 888-417-0195

Produced for Focus Readers by Red Line Editorial.

Photographs ©: Anton Petrus/Shutterstock Images, cover, 1; Janugio/iStockphoto, 4–5; Red Line Editorial, 6; mtcurado/iStockphoto, 8–9; rabbit75_ist/iStockphoto, 10–11, 29; WA van den Noort/Shutterstock Images, 12; apple2499/Shutterstock Images, 14; garytog/iStockphoto, 16–17; JackF/iStockphoto, 18, 22–23; Kyslynskyy/iStockphoto, 20; paulafrench/iStockphoto, 24 (top left); tryptophanatic/Shutterstock Images, 24 (top right); StuPorts/iStockphoto, 24 (bottom left); pjmalsbury/iStockphoto, 24 (bottom right); Png Studio Photography/Shutterstock Images, 26

ISBN
978-1-63517-262-1 (hardcover)
978-1-63517-327-7 (paperback)
978-1-63517-457-1 (ebook pdf)
978-1-63517-392-5 (hosted ebook)

Library of Congress Control Number: 2017935139

Printed in the United States of America
Mankato, MN
June, 2017

About the Author

Tammy Gagne has written more than 150 books for adults and children. She resides in northern New England with her husband and son. One of her favorite pastimes is visiting schools to talk to kids about the writing process.

TABLE OF CONTENTS

CHAPTER 1

COMING TOGETHER

A wild dog watches a gazelle raise its head. The gazelle had stopped for a quick drink. Now it is in danger. The dog runs after the lone gazelle. But the gazelle runs faster. In only seconds, it reaches safety.

Thomson's gazelles are the most common type of gazelle.

Africa

Indian
Ocean

Atlantic
Ocean

☐ where gazelles live

Many gazelles live in Africa. Some live in Asia.

African gazelles can live in
different **habitats**. Some of these
gazelles live in **savannas**. Others

live in the desert. One **species** lives in the mountains. These gazelles **migrate** to lower regions in the winter. During the dry season, some gazelles move north. They travel into the African bush. This large area contains a variety of plants and trees.

FUN FACT

The largest gazelle species is the dama gazelle. A Speke's gazelle is the smallest gazelle species.

SURVIVING DRY CLIMATES

Gazelles live in hot and dry areas. In these areas, even small amounts of water can keep animals healthy. Gazelles lose a small amount of water every time they **exhale**. But when it is very dry, they change the way they breathe. This allows them to lose even less water. By changing their breathing, gazelles can survive in the hottest and driest climates. Some can go their entire lives without drinking any water. They get all the water they need from the plants they eat.

Dorcas gazelles can live in the Sahara desert.

CHAPTER 2

LARGE AND SMALL

Gazelles are a type of **antelope**. They are thin and graceful. Gazelles look similar to deer. But they are more closely related to goats, cattle, and sheep. There are many species of gazelle.

A dama gazelle is white with red markings.

A group of Grant's gazelles gather in a field.

Each species of gazelle looks a bit

different. They can vary greatly in

size. Some adult gazelles are only 1.7 feet (0.5 m) tall. Others can grow to be as tall as 5.5 feet (1.7 m). The smallest gazelles can weigh only 26 pounds (12 kg). The largest species can reach up to 165 pounds (75 kg). Male gazelles are usually bigger than females.

FUN FACT

Some gazelle species have a black stripe on the sides of their bodies.

▷ Two Cuvier's gazelles fight with their horns.

Gazelles are mainly tan or reddish-brown. They have white

rumps. They may also have markings on their coats. These could be stripes or spots. Each species has different markings.

Both male and female gazelles have curved horns. Their horns have rings. The horns can grow up to 14 inches (36 cm) long.

Male gazelles have bigger horns than females do. Gazelles also use their horns against one another. Sometimes these animals play roughly.

CHAPTER 3

GETTING AWAY

Predators can easily spot gazelles on the savanna. But gazelles can run as fast as 40 miles per hour (64 km/h). They can run fast for long periods. This helps them escape from predators.

A gazelle tries to outrun a cheetah.

PARTS OF A GAZELLE

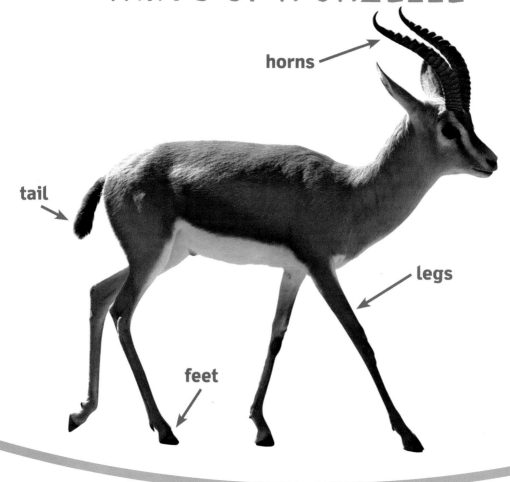

horns

tail

legs

feet

Gazelles often leap into the air. As they jump, they lift all four feet off the ground at once. This movement

is called pronking. Scientists are not sure why gazelles do this.

Some scientists believe pronking discourages predators from chasing gazelles. A gazelle may also use its horns to defend itself if a predator attacks. Common predators include cheetahs, lions, and wild dogs.

FUN FACT

A Thomson's gazelle can run as fast as 60 miles per hour (97 km/h) in short bursts.

 A gerenuk is the only gazelle species that can reach leaves without leaning on a tree.

Some gazelles can stand on their back legs. This helps them reach leaves on high tree branches. Some gazelles do not even have to lean on the tree. They are the only antelope species that can stand on their hind legs this way.

FUN FACT

Gazelles that live in the desert have wide hooves. These help them walk in sand.

CHAPTER 4

EVERYDAY LIFE

Gazelles are **social** animals. They use body language to communicate. Their movements have meanings. Flicking their tails or stomping their feet might warn others that a predator is nearby.

A herd of Thomson's gazelles lies down for a rest.

GAZELLE LIFE CYCLE

Female gazelles have one or two newborns at a time.

Newborns are called fawns.

When grown, they join a herd.

The mother hides the fawns from predators.

Gazelles live in groups called herds. Many herds are made up of all males or all females. Herds of gazelles join together when they begin their migration. A herd can have as few as 10 gazelles. It can have as many as 700 gazelles.

Living in a herd also helps gazelles. A predator is less likely to attack a group of gazelles than a single gazelle. Predators look for gazelles that wander too far from their herds.

A Speke's gazelle eats from a branch.

Gazelles are herbivores. This means they eat only plants. They eat mostly herbs and leaves. If

these are not available, they eat what they can find. Sometimes they eat grasses and shoots instead. Gazelles also eat fruit.

When they are migrating, gazelles follow zebras in hopes of finding food. The zebras eat the taller parts of the grass. Short, soft shoots are left behind. Gazelles can chew these easily.

FOCUS ON
GAZELLES

Write your answers on a separate sheet of paper.

1. Write a paragraph that explains the main ideas of Chapter 3.

2. Why do you think pronking discourages predators from chasing gazelles?

3. Which animals do gazelles follow when migrating?
   - A. deer
   - B. lions
   - C. zebras

4. What will a gazelle do if it sees a predator nearby?
   - A. It will run up to the predator and challenge it.
   - B. It will stand up on its hind legs to scare the predator.
   - C. It will stomp its feet to warn the other gazelles.

5. What does **shoots** mean in this book?

The zebras eat the taller parts of the grass. Short, soft shoots are left behind.

    A. parts of a plant

    B. groups of zebras

    C. ways of eating

6. What does **markings** mean in this book?

They may also have markings on their coats. These could be stripes or spots. Each species has different markings.

    A. patterns on an animal's coat

    B. animals that have no fur

    C. ways of moving through grass

Answer key on page 32.

GLOSSARY

antelope
A animal that lives in Africa and Asia and is related to cattle, goats, and sheep.

exhale
To release air by breathing it out of the body.

habitats
The type of places where plants or animals normally grow or live.

migrate
To move from one region to another at the change of the seasons.

predators
Animals that hunt other animals for food.

rumps
The back parts of animals' bodies.

savannas
Grasslands with few or no trees.

social
Likely to spend time with other animals of the same type.

species
A group of animals or plants that are similar.

TO LEARN MORE

BOOKS

Higgins, Melissa. *Grassland Ecosystems*. Mankato, MN: Abdo Publishing, 2016.

Meinking, Mary. *Lion vs. Gazelle*. Eustis, FL: Raintree, 2011.

Spelman, Lucy. *Animal Encyclopedia*. Washington, DC: National Geographic Kids, 2012.

NOTE TO EDUCATORS

Visit **www.focusreaders.com** to find lesson plans, activities, links, and other resources related to this title.

INDEX

Answer Key: 1. Answers will vary; **2.** Answers will vary; **3.** C; **4.** C; **5.** A; **6.** A